I ♥ TAYLOR SWIFT

UPDATED & EXPANDED VERSION

AN UNOFFICIAL FAN JOURNAL

*Obsess Over Your Favorite Lyrics,
Learn More Fascinating Facts about Taylor, &
Celebrate What It Means to Be a Swiftie!*

★ Includes *TTPD* ★

PRINCESS GABBARA

ADAMS MEDIA
New York   London   Toronto   Sydney   New Delhi

Aadamsmedia
Adams Media
An Imprint of Simon & Schuster, LLC
100 Technology Center Drive
Stoughton, Massachusetts 02072

This Adams Media hardcover edition November 2024
First Adams Media hardcover edition July 2023

ADAMS MEDIA and colophon are trademarks of Simon & Schuster, LLC.

Simon & Schuster: Celebrating 100 Years of Publishing in 2024

For information about special discounts for bulk purchases, please contact Simon & Schuster Special Sales at 1-866-506-1949 or business@simonandschuster.com.

The Simon & Schuster Speakers Bureau can bring authors to your live event. For more information or to book an event, contact the Simon & Schuster Speakers Bureau at 1-866-248-3049 or visit our website at www.simonspeakers.com.

Interior design by Priscilla Yuen
Interior illustrations by Indira Yuniarti
Interior images © 123RF; Simon & Schuster, LLC

Manufactured in the United States of America

1 2024

ISBN 978-1-5072-2378-9

CONTENTS

INTRODUCTION

Think back to when you first heard Taylor Swift sing. Did her lyrics seem to describe your life? Or even make you laugh sometimes? Were you blown away by her ability to put some seriously deep feelings into relatable songs that get stuck in your head for days? The multiple-Grammy-winning artist makes world domination look easy—and we Swifties have been there with her since day one!

Since her 2006 debut, Taylor has consistently been iconic, selling out massive stadiums around the globe and shattering records left and right, including dominating *Billboard*'s entire top 10 on its Hot 100 chart and having the most monthly Spotify listeners. Not to mention that her music videos for "Shake It Off" and "Blank Space" are among the most viewed YouTube videos of all time. But what we love most about Taylor is her skill for writing specific lyrics that detail her own experiences, but feel like she's talking about us. Plus, she can inspire you to be the best version of yourself! Let's be real: Her music is the soundtrack to our lives.

As you stream, support, and follow Taylor on the daily, fill in the pages of this book to capture all the ways she manages to slay day in and day out. Only you know exactly what Taylor Swift means to you—so use this journal to record how her music is a personal experience for you. You'll be given prompts to:

- ✏️ ▶ *Write about a time when Taylor's unapologetic lyrics gave you the courage to tell your own story.*

- ✏️ ▶ *Imagine winning a free meet and greet with Taylor if you belt out one of her tunes without messing up the lyrics. What song do you sing?*

- ✏️ ▶ *Journal about what's next for her by imagining who you would cast to play Taylor in her biopic if and when that day comes.*

Not only do you get fun prompts; this journal also tests your knowledge! You'll find trivia questions on a huge range of topics, challenging even the most devoted fan. In the back of the journal, there are also Taylor-themed coloring pages and space to make your own mini scrapbook. Paste in pics of the best looks Taylor has served up, handwrite lyrics you're vibing with right now, and make this journal your most treasured keepsake. Celebrate all the things you love about one of the most iconic queens in the world with *I Love Taylor Swift (Updated & Expanded Version)*!

Today, Taylor Swift is one of the most successful and prolific artists on the planet, but her achievements go beyond her awards and sales. With every business decision, she manages to leave the music industry a lot better than how she found it, paving the way for her peers and up-and-coming artists. Back in 2006, though, Taylor was a seventeen-year-old country musician on a mission to make a name for herself and hear her songs on the radio. A couple years prior to her debut, a Faith Hill documentary convinced Taylor she needed to uproot her life from Reading, Pennsylvania, and try her luck in Nashville. Eager to jump-start her dreams of making it big as a country music star, Taylor spent two years going to and from Music City, performing at local festivals, coffee shops, and industry showcases for anyone who'd listen.

In 2004, her hard work paid off when she caught the attention of DreamWorks Records executive Scott Borchetta, who at the time was forming his own label, Big Machine Records. Then, in June 2006, Taylor released "Tim McGraw," the lead single off her eponymous debut studio album, which spawned two number one hits ("Our Song" and "Should've Said No") on *Billboard*'s Hot Country Songs chart. As we know now, Taylor was just getting warmed up.

To keep the momentum going, Taylor released two EPs, *The Taylor Swift Holiday Collection* and *Beautiful Eyes*—the latter of which offered a preview of what was to come, as it featured a mostly country pop sound. In 2008, Taylor's highly anticipated sophomore album, *Fearless*, launched her first-ever headlining tour while inching her one step closer to crossover success. The next year, "You Belong with Me" took home Best Female Video at the MTV Video Music Awards (VMAs), proving that Taylor's fan base was growing exponentially despite a now-infamous interruption from rapper Kanye West. *Speak Now* (2010)—written entirely by Taylor—presented a more empowered version of the then-twenty-one-year-old country star.

Reminiscent of her idol Shania Twain's crossover success in the 1990s, Taylor made her full foray into pop music with *Red*. Lead single "We Are Never Ever Getting Back Together" became her first *Billboard* Hot 100 chart-topper, but it was 2014 that marked a pivotal year and musical rebirth for Taylor. Described as her first "official pop album," *1989* produced three number one hits: "Shake It Off," "Blank Space," and "Bad Blood." If there was any shred of doubt surrounding Taylor's willingness to take creative risks, *1989* proved that her vision and talent couldn't be confined to just one genre.

At that point, constant gossip surrounding Taylor's highly publicized relationships and feuds with other celebrities forced her to retreat from the spotlight. Like a true singer-songwriter, she poured those frustrations into her music, creating *Reputation*, her aptly titled sixth studio effort, which included the unforgettable comeback single "Look What You Made Me Do." The following year, 2019, Taylor made history when she became the most awarded artist in American Music Awards (AMAs) history. Talk about iconic!

Toward the end of her Reputation Stadium Tour, Taylor began recording *Lover*, her first album released following her departure from Big Machine Records. Trading in the sweet revenge heard on *Reputation* for a brighter, more whimsical sound, the album showcased her newfound artistic freedom. For the first time, Taylor tackled issues like feminism and LGBTQ+ rights in her music. She was also gearing up for the release of the movie version of *Cats*. When she was younger, Taylor had dreamed of being a Broadway star, so starring in the 2019 film adaptation of Andrew Lloyd Webber's hit stage musical of the same name definitely seemed like a full-circle moment. Then, during a global pandemic, Taylor surprised her fans by releasing two albums, *Folklore* and *Evermore*, five months apart from each other. When *Folklore* took home Album of the Year at the 2021 Grammy Awards, Taylor made headlines as the first woman to conquer the coveted category three times.

During the *Lover* era, Taylor found herself in a dispute with Big Machine Records when talent manager Scooter Braun acquired the label from Borchetta and sold Taylor's masters for $300 million. Instead of staying silent, Taylor announced in 2019 that she was rerecording her first six albums, starting with

Fearless, then *Red*. Her ten-minute version of "All Too Well" even made history as the longest song to top the *Billboard* Hot 100.

Fast-forward to 2024: Taylor boasts back-to-back multiplatinum-selling studio albums, including *Midnights* and *The Tortured Poets Department* (aka *TTPD*). These concept albums display her innermost thoughts and ooze a level of artistic expression and confidence that simply cannot be taught. What's more, the albums broke multiple Spotify records—giving her bragging rights as the most-streamed artist on the platform, and first place for having the most pre-saves ever!

On top of that, the Eras Tour took on a life of its own when it kicked off in the summer of 2023. The extravaganza was filled with unforgettable moments that live rent-free in our minds. Swifties will never forget when Taylor announced that *Speak Now* and *1989* would be her next rerecordings or when ex Taylor Lautner joined her onstage and did a backflip! Not only did the Eras Tour remind the world of Taylor's greatness, as it touched on every one of her incredible "eras"—it also gave the US economy an estimated $5 billion boost! Now, that is truly the definition of "epic."

At this point in her illustrious career, it's exciting to think about what Taylor could dream up next! With millions of records sold and hundreds of awards won, Taylor has nothing left to prove, and yet she is just as enthusiastic about creating great music as she was when she was still a newcomer. Taylor's reign is just beginning...

PART

" *Enchanted* "

Named after some of Taylor's most beloved
songs, each chapter in this part explores what
makes her such a gem among her peers and
loyal fans. Whether it's discussing her impact on
the way streaming platforms operate or reveling
in the thought of spending an entire day with her
in your hometown, you'll lose yourself in it all,
while geeking out whenever you answer a trivia
question correctly along the way. Get ready to
become more and more "Enchanted" by Taylor's
music and lyrical know-how in the pages ahead.

ONE

"BLANK SPACE"

TAYLOR SWIFT is one of the great songwriters of her generation. You don't just listen to her music; you can really feel and envision every lyric and note. Taylor truly transforms every "Blank Space" into songs with stories that have the power to captivate us. Through her lyrical content, we've learned a lot about the highs and lows that helped shape Taylor into the artist and person she is today. From her genius metaphors to her ability to paint pictures with words, this chapter is all about celebrating the smash hits, albums, and sincere storytelling that have propelled Taylor to the top of the charts.

Which is your absolute favorite and least favorite Taylor album? Rank her entire discography from best to worst, and write a few lines next to each album explaining your decision.

Which songs do you think give the most insight into Taylor's personality? What about your personality? Why did you choose these specific songs?

Taylor has written hundreds of masterpieces. What song do you wish you could hear again for the first time? What memories do you associate with the song?

Taylor is among the artists who boast the most charted songs on the *Billboard* Hot 100. What song of hers do you think deserves more hype? Why did you choose this song? What aspects about it get overlooked?

```
╭─────────────────────────────────────────╮
│                                           │
│        _____        │
│              SONG TITLE                   │
╰─────────────────────────────────────────╯
```

1989 is Taylor's highest-selling album to date. Which of her studio albums is the most meaningful to you? What's your favorite track on the album?

MOST MEANINGFUL STUDIO ALBUM

FAVORITE TRACK

In 2019, Taylor announced that rerecordings of her first six albums were underway. What was your initial reaction upon hearing the exciting news? Do you prefer any of the rerecorded songs to the original recordings?

Which *Fearless* song earned
Taylor her first-ever
Grammy Award in 2010?

A "Love Story"

B "You Belong with Me"

C "White Horse"

D "Fifteen"

My Answer

Ice Spice, Post Malone, Lana Del Rey—everyone wants to work with Taylor! Which of her collabs surprised you the most? Who is your favorite featured artist? And what makes their track with Taylor an absolute banger?

From slowly revealing the track list through "Midnights Mayhem with Me" to the surprise MTV VMAs announcement, Taylor had plenty of tricks up her sleeve in the weeks leading up to the release of *Midnights*. What did you enjoy most about the album's rollout? Anything you'd change? Any out-of-the-box ideas that could've been a hit?

Whenever Taylor and Ed Sheeran link up musically, it's perfection! What's your favorite song of theirs? How do you think their songwriting abilities complement each other? Do you think they will pair up again in the near future? Is there anything new or different you'd like to hear them try next time?

_____

_____

_____

_____

_____

_____

_____

Let's say an alien lands on Earth and has never heard Taylor's music. What song or album do you suggest they listen to first? Why do you feel this song or album is the best representation of Taylor?

_____

_____

_____

_____

_____

_____

_____

_____

Taylor has penned numerous tunes for other artists, including Miley Cyrus, Sugarland, and Little Big Town. What artist should Taylor write a song for next? Why did you choose this artist?

With 2012's *Red*, Taylor shifted toward more of a pop sound, as evidenced in "I Knew You Were Trouble" and "22." What music style should she explore next? What can she bring to this genre?

Which of Taylor's songs
narrowly missed the number
one spot on the *Billboard*
Hot 100?

A "We Are Never Ever Getting
Back Together"

B "Bad Blood"

C "You Need to Calm Down"

D "Down Bad"

My Answer

Taylor's lyrics usually stem from real-life experiences. What song do you wish you knew the full story behind? Using your Swiftie knowledge, what do you think inspired the tune?

SONG TITLE

Jot down the five Taylor lyrics you love most.

ONE

TWO

THREE

FOUR

FIVE

Taylor's talent for singing and writing her own songs makes her a queen in the music industry. Which one of her rhymes really slays?

RHYME

Listening to Taylor's entire catalog will keep you busy for hours. If you could only listen to one of her albums for the rest of your life, which one would you choose and why?

ALBUM TITLE

Taylor pulls out all the stops when it comes to her remixes. Which hit single deserves to be reimagined? What would you change about the track?

HIT SINGLE

_____

_____

_____

_____

_____

_____

Which are your top five favorite remixes that Taylor's done so far?

ONE _____

TWO _____

THREE _____

FOUR _____

FIVE _____

The Eras Tour featured "Cruel Summer" early on in the set list, causing the song to go viral and re-enter the *Billboard* Hot 100 chart. Four years after its initial release, it stayed number one for four weeks. What's another song by Taylor that deserves a similar resurgence? What do you love about it?

SONG TITLE

Midnights and *The Tortured Poets Department* are considered among Taylor's most personal albums. Between the extended versions of *Midnights* and *TTPD*, Taylor released more than fifty songs! Which five tracks best represent her personal growth?

1
2
3
4
5

Taylor's storytelling has grown by leaps and bounds. Thinking all the way back to her 2006 debut album, what's the biggest difference you've noticed in her lyrical prowess? What impresses you the most? How do you think she'll continue to evolve as a songwriter?

_____

_____

_____

_____

_____

_____

_____

_____

_____

_____

Jack Antonoff is Taylor's go-to writing partner. "Sweeter Than Fiction" in 2013 marked their first collab. What do you think Jack brings to Taylor's artistry? What's the best song they've written together?

```
┌─────────────────────────────────────┐
│                                       │
│  _____    │
│             SONG TITLE                │
└─────────────────────────────────────┘
```

_____

_____

_____

_____

Taylor likes sharing behind-the-scenes info on the creative process. If you could sit in on any studio session, which would you choose and why?

STUDIO SESSION

When Taylor was twelve years old, a computer repairman taught her how to play the guitar. What's the first song she learned?

A "Breathe"
by **FAITH HILL**

B "You're Still the One"
by **SHANIA TWAIN**

C "Kiss Me"
by **SIXPENCE NONE THE RICHER**

D "Barely Breathing"
by **DUNCAN SHEIK**

My Answer

"'Cause baby now we got bed bugs" and "All the lonely Starbucks lovers" are just a couple of lyrics people thought they heard. What are the funniest lyrics you've misheard in Taylor's songs over the years? Jot them down.

Taylor's album covers are constantly evolving to reflect her personal growth and ever-changing musical identity. What cover do you think best captures Taylor's essence?

ALBUM COVER

While you're at it, rank your top five favorite album covers.

ONE

TWO

THREE

FOUR

FIVE

Did you know Taylor grew up on a Christmas tree farm? In 2007, Taylor released her six-track Christmas EP featuring classics like "Last Christmas" and "Santa Baby." Should Taylor put out a full Christmas album? If that happens, what other holiday tunes should she sing?

_____

_____

_____

_____

_____

_____

_____

_____

The vinyl versions of Taylor's studio albums have sold millions of copies, solidifying her vinyl queen status. Have you ever heard a vinyl record played? If so, which of Taylor's studio albums would sound the best spinning on a record player?

(_____

STUDIO ALBUM)

_____

_____

_____

_____

Taylor's first single, "Tim McGraw," debuted in the spring of 2006. What's the first song by Taylor you ever heard? Do you remember where you were, what you were doing, and who you were with? Was it love at first listen, or did you grow to like it later?

SONG TITLE

Which of Taylor's albums did
not win a Grammy Award for
Album of the Year?

(A) *Red*

(B) *1989*

(C) *Fearless*

(D) *Folklore*

My Answer

No one writes a prologue quite like Taylor. Her honest words instantly capture your interest and have a way of making you feel even closer to the music. Which album prologue do you love the most?

_____
ALBUM TITLE

_____

_____

_____

_____

_____

Taylor goes out of her way to share with her fans the inspiration behind every album she records. Which of her albums has the most interesting backstory?

_____
ALBUM TITLE

_____

_____

_____

_____

_____

Taylor and Lana Del Rey's *Midnights* collab, "Snow on the Beach," was long awaited, but appearances from Zoë Kravitz and Dylan O'Brien were delightful surprises. What do you think of their contributions? Were you previously aware of their musical talents?

Taylor's "3am" deluxe edition of *Midnights* features seven bonus tracks. Do any of them come close to outshining the original songs? Based on the titles alone, which one is the most intriguing to you?

At the 2022 Toronto International Film Festival, Taylor revealed that the missing red scarf in "All Too Well" is actually a metaphor. What other metaphors have you identified in Taylor's music? Write down as many as you can think of.

All of Taylor's lead singles set the tone for what the Swifties can expect from each new and exciting era. Which one do you think makes the strongest statement?

LEAD SINGLE

Rank your top five favorite lead singles.

ONE

TWO

THREE

FOUR

FIVE

With *Midnights*, Taylor returned to electronic pop, as heard on *1989*. Were you surprised by the musical direction she took with this album? Did it live up to your expectations? What's your favorite track of the bunch? Which took the longest to grow on you?

CHAPTER TWO

"STYLE"

WHEN TAYLOR BURST onto the music scene in 2006, fans lived for her songwriting abilities right away, and it wasn't long before her "Style" took center stage as well. Whether it's bringing her beloved songs to life with stunning visuals and electric performances or rocking the perfect fit while accepting her millionth award, Tay Tay's look always slays. Part of the journey toward achieving icon status is having live music to back it up—and that's where her concerts and tours come in. Get ready to replay Taylor's most memorable looks in her music videos, concerts, red carpet appearances, and more in this chapter.

From "Drops of Jupiter" to "Bette Davis Eyes," Taylor enjoys covering iconic songs during her live shows. Which is your favorite? What song do you want to hear covered next? How does the song you chose fit in with Taylor's vibe?

_____

_____

_____

_____

_____

_____

_____

_____

Fans were psyched when Taylor performed "Ronan" at her 1989 Tour. What song that she hasn't performed live do you want to hear one of these days?

SONG TITLE

_____

_____

_____

_____

When it comes to touring, Taylor never fails to wow her fans. Design your dream set list, including any ideas for stage costumes, cover songs, and guest stars.

Taylor has directed many of her own music videos. Which one earned Taylor her first solo directing credit?

A "I'm Only Me When I'm with You"

B "The Best Day"

C "Mine"

D "The Man"

My Answer

Visually speaking, "You Need to Calm Down," "The Man," and "Bejeweled" are among Taylor's most memorable videos. What song deserves its own music video? What director would you enlist to bring your vision to life? Describe your concept.

SONG TITLE

From her street style to slaying on the red carpet, Taylor knows how to make a statement. What do you appreciate about her style evolution? How would you sum up her aesthetic? Do you think she should take more fashion risks? What would you suggest?

_____

_____

_____

_____

_____

_____

_____

_____

_____

_____

Does the 2016 Met Gala futuristic dress take your number one spot—or is it the vibrant orange and pink two-piece number Taylor rocked at the 2016 Grammys? Which red carpet looks deserve a place in her top five?

ONE

TWO

THREE

FOUR

FIVE

Taylor has performed at all the major awards shows, including the Grammys, the *Billboard* Music Awards, and the BRIT Awards. What performance do you think best represents Taylor's vibe? Do you think she gets enough credit as a performer?

PERFORMANCE

People love dressing up as their favorite celebrities for Halloween. If Halloween is your thing, which of Taylor's outfits would you be most excited to re-create? How would you make it your own? Write about or draw it here.

Following the release of her debut album, Taylor performed as the opening act for which country artist?

A Rascal Flatts

B Keith Urban

C Tim McGraw and Faith Hill

D All of the above

My Answer

ANSWER D. Taylor also opened for George Strait and Brad Paisley to help promote her debut album.

51

Taylor's Eras Tour is the highest-grossing tour that's ever existed. Did you score tickets? What do you remember most about the experience? What was the highlight of the show? Were you sobbing? What merch did you pick up? Who did you bring along?

_____

_____

_____

_____

_____

_____

_____

_____

_____

_____

Have you been lucky enough to see Taylor five times in person? If so, rank those concerts here. If not, rank any shows you have been to, along with any other live performances you've watched her rock.

ONE

TWO

THREE

FOUR

FIVE

Taylor is no stranger to turning heads—whether she's giving gorgeous vibes in a custom floral mini dress at the 2021 Grammys or serving up looks like a yellow pastel suit in her "Me!" music video. If you could create a brand-new aesthetic for Taylor, what event would it be for? Design a new fit here.

Every time Taylor attends the Met Gala, you can count on her to make jaws drop. What year marked her debut?

A 2007   **C** 2010

B 2008   **D** 2013

My Answer

ANSWER B. On the heels of her sophomore LP, Fearless, Taylor made her first Met Gala appearance in 2008.

54

Taylor has graced the covers of countless magazines. Map out your dream concept for a photo shoot for your favorite magazine. Would she have designer drip? If so, what are her brands?

Taylor passed on headlining the 2023 Super Bowl halftime show. If she ever decides to perform at the Super Bowl, what songs should she include in her set list? What guest stars should she bring out?

Seeing Taylor perform live in concert is a bucket list dream for many Swifties. Have you ever been shouted out by Taylor at one of her concerts? Draw a concert sign that'll get you noticed in a crowd.

Taylor premiered *All Too Well: The Short Film* at the 2022 Toronto International Film Festival. Which of Taylor's hits or lesser-known songs deserves a short film? Describe every element of this story, from the plot and the actors to any potential Easter eggs.

_____

_____

_____

_____

_____

_____

_____

_____

_____

Which fits that Taylor has worn while performing stand out most to you? Do you prefer sparkles and bright colors, understated glamour, or a punk look? List your top five stage costumes here.

_____

_____

ONE	
TWO	
THREE	
FOUR	
FIVE	

Taylor's Eras Tour was one for the books! Do you plan to attend her next concert? Draw the perfect outfit you'd wear.

The *All Too Well* short film is a perfect example of Taylor's range of talents. With Taylor set to make her directorial debut in the near future, what kind of stories should she bring to the big screen?

Taylor loves bringing out special guests during her concerts and even performing a duet with some of them. Which artist should join Taylor onstage next? What song should they perform together?

The number of celebrities who've popped up in Taylor's music videos over the years is seemingly endless. Who's been your favorite guest star and why?

MY FAVORITE GUEST STAR

It's probably very hard to narrow down—but which music videos would you put in Taylor's top five?

ONE

TWO

THREE

FOUR

FIVE

Taylor appreciates a good cardigan sweater—she even has a song named after this article of clothing! Do you have the *Folklore*-branded cardigan? Draw your own cardigan design you think would impress Taylor.

Taylor's music videos are like mini movies with captivating storylines from start to finish. Which video deserves a sequel? What cool ideas do you have for taking the story to the next level?

```
╭──────────────────────────────────────────╮
│                                            │
│      _____      │
│               MUSIC VIDEO                  │
╰──────────────────────────────────────────╯
```

Dozens of famous faces showed up to surprise fans at Taylor's 1989 Tour. Which artist didn't crash the party?

A Alanis Morissette

B John Legend

C Future

D Miranda Lambert

My Answer

In 2020, at Global Citizen's *One World: Together at Home* TV special, Taylor fought back tears as she performed "Soon You'll Get Better," a country ballad featuring the Chicks that was inspired by her mother Andrea's cancer battle. Which of Taylor's performances brings you to tears every time you watch it? Why?

MUSIC VIDEO

_____

_____

_____

_____

_____

_____

_____

_____

_____

_____

_____

_____

_____

_____

_____

_____

_____

_____

Taylor's *1989* reflects the year she was born—plus, the music was heavily influenced by 1980s synth-pop. Do you know any good tunes from the year Taylor was born? Re-create Taylor's *1989* Polaroids customized with your own initials and birth year, and **tape** it in the box on this page.

In 2022, Taylor spoke at New York University's (NYU's) commencement ceremony, where she also received an honorary doctorate in fine arts. Her speech (look it up!) was full of wisdom and life hacks, but what about her remarks resonates with you the most?

The Swifties who appear in Taylor's "Shake It Off" music video were brought in as a surprise. After busting a move with Taylor, they vowed to keep it under wraps until after the video dropped. If you could appear in any of Taylor's videos, which would it be and why?

Music icons like Mariah Carey, Britney Spears, and Adele have all held a Las Vegas residency, where they perform at the same location for at least several weeks. Do you think Taylor should do the same? Why or why not? Brainstorm a fun name for her residency.

_____

_____

_____

_____

_____

_____

_____

Fearless marked the launch of Taylor's first headlining tour with Gloriana and Kellie Pickler as opening acts. What artist(s) would you like to see open on her next tour?

_____

_____

_____

_____

_____

_____

_____

_____

In which city of the Eras Tour did Taylor receive an eight-minute standing ovation that made her tear up?

A Los Angeles

B Las Vegas

C Nashville

D Chicago

My Answer

ANSWER A. "I'm going to spend several decades trying to figure out words for how that just made me feel," Taylor told the audience.

Many Swifties travel to see Taylor perform live. Have you ever booked a flight just to see Tay Tay rock the stage? How far did you go? Was it your first time there? Did you turn it into a mini vacation? If you haven't gone anywhere yet, where would you *like* to go?

LOCATION

Taylor Swift: The Eras Tour is the highest-grossing concert film in history. Did you see it in theaters? If you saw the concert in person, how did it compare to the movie? What moments did you enjoy reliving the most on the big screen?

Taylor has admitted she's scared to perform at Coachella. Do you think she should perform at the iconic festival? In one hundred words or less, try to convince Taylor why she'd be great as a Coachella headliner.

Whenever Taylor rocks the stage, her ensembles are just as amazing as her performances! Which costume do you live for? Describe it here.

Taylor flexed her acting skills in a handful of movies, with 2010's *Valentine's Day* and 2019's *Cats* being her most memorable. How would you rate Taylor as an actress? Going forward, do you think she should continue to explore acting?

During her NYU commencement speech, Taylor joked about dressing like a 1950s housewife "for the entirety of 2012." If you could raid Taylor's closet, what fits would you put on first?

CHAPTER THREE

"EYES OPEN"

IF YOU'VE BEEN A SWIFTIE LONG ENOUGH, then you know there's more than what meets the eye with Taylor's music videos, social media posts, liner notes, date nights, and even her fashion choices. No one else creates a little mystery like Taylor, which is why it pays to keep your "Eyes Open." One of two songs penned for *The Hunger Games* movie soundtrack, it reminds listeners that there's always more under the surface if you look hard enough. With that theme in mind, prepare to channel your inner detective in this chapter as you revisit the hidden messages and surprises Taylor's become so known for.

According to Taylor, there are thousands of Easter eggs in the music video for "Look What You Made Me Do." List everything you've spotted so far.

Taylor's made a ton of music videos. Select one of your favorites, and write down several Easter eggs she could have used. What are they, and why did you choose these hidden messages to include?

_____

_____

_____

_____

_____

_____

_____

_____

_____

Which five of Taylor's many Easter eggs do you think are the most creative, fun, or unique?

ONE _____

TWO _____

THREE _____

FOUR _____

FIVE _____

Taylor goes to great lengths to thwart the paparazzi, from walking backward to supposedly traveling inside a giant suitcase. Which evasion moment was her most iconic?

Taylor shocked fans when she announced at the 2024 Grammys that *The Tortured Poets Department* was arriving sooner than anyone expected. What's the biggest surprise Taylor has ever pulled off?

Which of Taylor's tracks contains "Life is full of little interruptions" as its hidden message?

- **A** "Cold As You"
- **B** "The Lucky One"
- **C** "Innocent"
- **D** "Out of the Woods"

My Answer

Up until *Reputation*, Taylor's liner notes contained hidden messages. For each song, the lyrics are lowercase except for each letter of the hidden message—though she did the opposite for *1989*. What is your favorite hidden message?

_____

_____

_____

_____

_____

_____

_____

_____

_____

Jot down which five liner notes in Taylor's hidden messages you found the most imaginative and fun.

ONE _____

TWO _____

THREE _____

FOUR _____

FIVE _____

Taylor is truly a marketing mastermind. Do you prefer her surprise announcements or traditional rollouts? List the pros and cons of both.

PREFERRED MARKETING TECHNIQUE

SURPRISE ANNOUNCEMENTS

TRADITIONAL ROLLOUTS

Several college courses are dedicated to critical discussions of Taylor's lyrical content. Would you sign up for the class? What songs would you want to examine specifically? Which of Taylor's metaphors do you like the most?

A lot of people are not aware of the fact that Taylor was named after James Taylor or that she has double-jointed elbows. Can you list other little-known facts about Taylor that may surprise other Swifties?

It's safe to say that Swifties will still be talking about the red scarf in "All Too Well" for many years to come. Which Easter eggs are just as brilliant but not discussed enough?

_____

_____

_____

_____

_____

_____

_____

_____

_____

_____

_____

In 2022, Taylor was featured as a puzzle on a *Wheel of Fortune* episode. Can you guess the three words used to describe Taylor?

The Taylor-themed iteration of Wordle—Taylordle—exploded in early 2022. Can you come up with five-letter words related to Taylor or her songs? Write them all here.

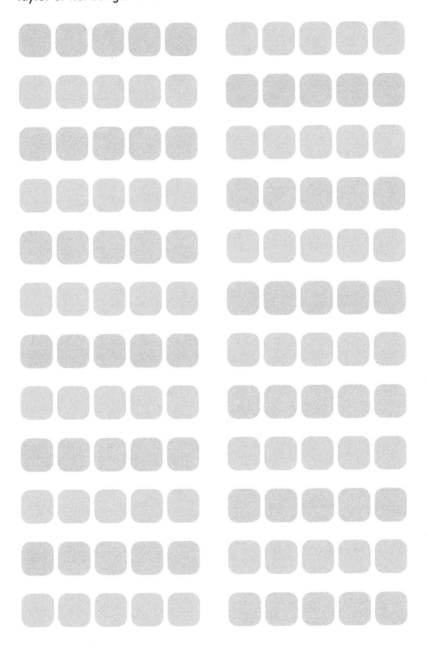

Taylor is a blazing Sagittarius. With astrology in mind, what zodiac signs do you think she's most compatible with in the love department? How do you think those signs would complement each other?

Taylor's relationship with NFL star Travis Kelce took the world by storm! It also marked Taylor's first time publicly dating an athlete. When you think about their coupledom, what are some of the biggest differences you noticed about Taylor's demeanor?

The top tier of the wedding cake showcased in the "I Bet You Think about Me" music video is covered in numbers. Which pair of numbers appear?

A 4 and 13 **C** 13 and 26

B 7 and 13 **D** 17 and 28

My Answer

The massive wedding cake in the "I Bet You Think about Me" video looks beautiful before Taylor takes a huge chunk out of it with her hand. If Taylor ever gets married, do you think her wedding cake will be lavish or more low-key? Draw a wedding cake design for her special day that's almost too pretty to eat.

When you're as famous as Taylor, the world watches your every move, so it's only natural for her to keep certain things to herself. If you were Taylor, what sort of things would you like to keep private? Your vacation locations? Your trips to the recording studio? Your workouts or date nights?

Since engagement rumors always seem to swirl around Taylor, dream up the perfect wedding for her, including the location, theme, guest list, and DJ.

_____

_____

_____

_____

_____

_____

_____

_____

_____

_____

Speaking of weddings, if you could have your first dance to any one of Taylor's songs, what would it be? What inspired your choice?

(
_____

SONG TITLE
)

_____

_____

_____

_____

_____

_____

Taylor and Joe Alwyn called it quits in 2023, but they dated each other for six years! During that time, they wrote six songs together. What do you think about their creative chemistry? What's your favorite track they penned?

FAVORITE TRACK

Joe Alwyn wrote songs with Taylor under the pseudonym William Bowery, inspired by his great-grandfather and the area of New York where he spent a lot of time. If you had to write a song with Taylor, what alias would you choose, and what's the inspiration behind it?

MY ALIAS

Using the subtle and sometimes not-so-subtle clues Taylor drops in her songs, videos, and social media posts, piece together a mini timeline for her current relationship.

_____

_____

_____

_____

_____

_____

_____

_____

_____

Taylor once revealed a hilarious secret from her pre-fame days: She used to drive past her ex-boyfriends' houses. Write down a funny secret you'd confess to Taylor if you had the chance.

_____

_____

_____

_____

_____

_____

_____

_____

_____

Which of Taylor's music videos features ex Joe Alwyn's name in Chinese calligraphy?

A "...Ready for It?"

B "Delicate"

C "I Don't Wanna Live Forever"

D "End Game"

My Answer

Although "Karma" is the eleventh track off *Midnights*, many Swifties are convinced there's a "lost" album Taylor never released, titled *Karma*, from 2016. Do you think the secret project exists? Why or why not? What are all the clues, if any, that suggest *Karma* is real? State your case for or against the theory.

With her 2020 albums *Folklore* and *Evermore*, Taylor drew from fictional characters and stories instead of her personal life for the first time. What do you think of this approach? Would you like to see Taylor continue down this path of creative experimentation?

Which music video features the title of its accompanying album written in the background of a scene?

A "Style"

B "Look What You Made Me Do"

C "22"

D "Me!"

My Answer

ANSWER D. Featuring Panic! At The Disco's Brendon Urie, "Me!" ushered in Taylor's Lover era.

They say a broken heart can spark creativity. Which one of Taylor's breakups do you think inspired her best work? What song do you think best speaks to the relationship? How do you think the breakup affected Taylor?

Taylor has enjoyed a few high-profile relationships over the years. Which pairing do you think didn't work out due to bad timing and/ or other external factors? What's your reasoning?

Taylor is known for inviting a carefully selected group of Swifties to her various homes across the US and the UK, where they can listen to an album before it is released. If her team invited you to one of these secret sessions, how would you react?

_____

_____

_____

_____

_____

_____

_____

_____

_____

Some fan theories make perfect sense, while others are a little... out there and take more convincing. List five here that have you fully invested.

ONE _____

TWO _____

THREE _____

FOUR _____

FIVE _____

Taylor's eleventh studio album, *The Tortured Poets Department*, ended up being a double album with a whopping thirty-one tracks! Were you surprised at the number of songs Taylor dropped? Did you spot any clues ahead of time? Share them here.

_____

_____

_____

_____

_____

_____

_____

_____

_____

Taylor makes zero apologies about drawing musical inspiration from her real-life romances. Which ex inspired the most interesting material, in your opinion? What are some of the most telling lyrics from that relationship?

_____

_____

_____

_____

_____

_____

_____

_____

Taylor announced *1989 (Taylor's Version)* at the Eras Tour while rocking a blue dress, which matters because she donned a blue dress in the "Out of the Woods" video from *1989*. What other Easter eggs have you spotted that signal what could be next for Taylor?

_____

_____

_____

_____

_____

_____

_____

_____

Ahead of *The Tortured Poets Department*, fans immersed themselves in a library pop-up tied to the album. Easter eggs included typewriters, bookshelves, clocks, and statues. What's another album of Taylor's that should receive a similar treatment? What props would you choose and why?

_____
ALBUM TITLE

_____

_____

_____

_____

Famous exes have inspired a lot of Taylor's lyrical content, but do you know the stories behind some of her most iconic breakup tracks? For each song, write down the guy who inspired it, as well as what's believed to have happened.

♪ "Picture to Burn"

♪ "Teardrops on My Guitar"

♪ "Better Than Revenge"

♪ "Mine"

♪ "The Story of Us"

♪ "Back to December"

♪ "You're Losing Me"

♪ "My Boy Only Breaks His Favorite Toys"

CHAPTER FOUR

"WILDEST DREAMS"

EVERY SWIFTIE HOPES they can meet their idol Taylor someday. Imagine getting to hang out with her! Whether you've wondered what life would be like as a member of her famous squad or daydreamed about being invited to one of her epic dinner parties, this chapter is dedicated to your "Wildest Dreams" and then some. In these next few pages, you'll get to show all the ways you live for Taylor, from the moment you became a Swiftie to dreaming up the best birthday celebration she's ever had. Are you Taylor's number one fan? Now's your chance to prove it.

Circa 2015, Taylor and her squad were stunning in her "Bad Blood" music video. What would you do if you could hang out with Taylor and her friends for a day? What fun or unique quality would you bring to the group?

_____

_____

_____

_____

_____

_____

_____

_____

_____

Taylor loves hanging out with the Swifties! If you were in Taylor's presence and you could only ask her one question, what would it be and why? What do you think her answer would be?

_____

_____

_____

_____

_____

_____

_____

_____

?

Which member of Taylor's squad appears first in the Joseph Kahn–directed "Bad Blood" music video?

A Gigi Hadid

B Zendaya

C Selena Gomez

D Cara Delevingne

My Answer

ANSWER C. Selena, whose friendship with Taylor dates back to 2008, nabbed the lead role of Arsyn.

From Nashville, Tennessee, to Beverly Hills, California, Taylor calls multiple cities home. Where's home for you? If you could spend an entire day with Taylor in your hometown, where's the first place you'd go? What made you choose this place? Write about why she'd love your hometown.

Taylor's 2020 *Miss Americana* documentary offers fans a glimpse into her personal life. What were your biggest takeaways? What, if anything, surprised you? What's one topic you wish Taylor addressed more?

Taylor loves interacting with the Swifties online and in real life. If you're one of the lucky ones who've met Taylor, describe your experience. Where did it happen? How did you react? Did you snap a selfie? What do you remember most?

_____

_____

_____

_____

_____

_____

_____

_____

_____

Taylor started playing the guitar when she was a preteen and is even credited for the rise in guitar sales among women. If you received guitar lessons from Taylor, which song of hers would you like to learn to play first and why?

```
   _____

                SONG TITLE
```

_____

_____

_____

_____

Taylor is known for hosting dinner parties packed with celebs. If you were lucky enough to score an invite, who would be your plus-one? What dish would you bring?

When Taylor's not busy crafting the perfect melodies, she loves to bake and visit antique shops. Do you and Taylor share similar interests? Have you adopted any of her hobbies as your own? Which hobbies of yours would you like to introduce her to?

If you haven't met Taylor, list five of the most amazing stories of *other* fans who've met the queen herself.

1

2

3

4

5

Inspired by her favorite TV shows and movies, the names of Taylor's cats are anything but basic. If Taylor tasks you with choosing a namesake for a new addition to her feline family, what are you going with?

Cardigan sweaters and the number thirteen are just a few of Taylor's favorite things. Can you quickly rattle off "22" of the superstar's other favorite things?

1

2

3

4

5

6

7

8

9

10

11

12

13

14

15

16

17

18

19

20

21

22

Imagine you're throwing a surprise birthday party for Taylor. What's the theme? What does the menu look like? What music would you play? What style of decorations would you set up? Write out every detail of this perfect birthday bash.

_____

_____

_____

_____

_____

_____

_____

_____

_____

If you could present Taylor with one gift on her birthday, December 13, what would it be? What made you choose this item?

_____

_____

_____

_____

_____

_____

_____

_____

_____

The cat backpack seen in Taylor's *Miss Americana* documentary went viral. Which one of her cats was she carrying while boarding a private jet?

A Meredith **C** Phoebe

B Olivia **D** Benjamin

My Answer

Taylor's "Bad Blood" music video features an all-star cast, including some of Taylor's famous besties. Using just your memory, can you write out every celebrity who makes a cameo in the order they appear?

Taylor's epic squad includes Jaime King, Hailee Steinfeld, and, of course, Selena Gomez. Who isn't in Taylor's circle but seems like they'd fit in perfectly?

Which five of Taylor's besties do you wish were your friends too?

ONE

TWO

THREE

FOUR

FIVE

Imagine this: You win a free meet and greet with Taylor if you belt out one of her tunes without messing up the lyrics. What song are you singing?

```
╭─────────────────────────────────────────╮
│                                           │
│  ───────────────────────────────────────  │
│              SONG TITLE                   │
╰─────────────────────────────────────────╯
```

_____

_____

_____

_____

_____

_____

Every Swiftie has their own story of how and when they became part of the fandom. What's yours? Was there a certain song, album, or moment that reeled you in?

_____

_____

_____

_____

_____

_____

_____

_____

_____

Taylor shelled out over $55 million in bonuses to her crew during the Eras Tour. If you had the chance to join Taylor's team, what job would you sign up for? Stylist, makeup artist, publicist, assistant, chef, security, cat sitter? Why are you perfect for the gig? What do you think it's like working with Taylor?

JOB TITLE

Lots of Swifties went the DIY route by making friendship bracelets to give each other at the Eras Tour shows. If you could gift a friendship bracelet to Taylor, what design would it have and what would it say? Why would you choose this message?

```
                MESSAGE
```

_____

_____

_____

_____

_____

_____

While performing "22" during the Eras Tour, Taylor handpicked one lucky Swiftie to receive an autographed fedora hat. Many fans say Taylor's mom, Andrea, scans the crowd and selects someone beforehand. What would you do to increase your chances of getting noticed?

_____

_____

_____

_____

_____

_____

_____

Even the most casual Taylor fans know that thirteen is her lucky number. List thirteen reasons why you can't get enough of the talented megastar.

1

2

3

4

5

6

7

8

9

10

11

12

13

?

Zodiac signs are determined by your exact time of birth. Taylor is a freedom-loving Sagittarius! What exact time was she born?

A 4:06 a.m.　　**C** 7:49 p.m.

B 5:17 a.m.　　**D** 11:23 p.m.

My Answer

From cozy hoodies and snuggly blankets to a dupe of the "All Too Well" red scarf, Taylor doesn't disappoint when it comes to merch. What piece do you treasure (and use) the most? Design your own merch idea here.

Taylor doesn't have any tattoos, but she once stated that if she ever got one, she'd settle on the number thirteen for obvious reasons. Do you like tattoos? If you got a tattoo honoring Taylor (or a "Taytoo," as the Swifties say), what lyrics or symbol would you select?

_____

_____

_____

_____

_____

_____

_____

_____

Some Swifties save old ticket stubs, backstage passes, and magazine clippings. What does your personal collection consist of? What item are you most proud of? What items are still on your wish list?

_____

_____

_____

_____

_____

_____

_____

_____

From baking cookies to unwrapping presents on Christmas Eve, Taylor's holiday traditions are a festive reminder that she's just like us! If you celebrate Christmas, what's a tradition you and your loved ones have that you think Taylor would enjoy?

_____

_____

_____

_____

_____

_____

_____

_____

_____

Taylor first showed off her acting chops in a 2009 episode of *CSI*, playing a troubled teenager. What TV show would you like to see Taylor guest-star on? Create the perfect role for her.

_____

_____

_____

_____

_____

_____

_____

_____

_____

Fan art of Taylor is always super-impressive. Have you ever immortalized Taylor through art? Even if art isn't your strong suit, try drawing a picture of Taylor from your favorite era.

In 2016, Taylor famously ditched the glamorous Met Gala after-parties to grab pizza with her squad while donning animal onesies. If Taylor invited you to a post–Met Gala slumber party, what onesie pajamas are you sporting? What fun activities would you suggest... Truth or Dare? Karaoke?

_____

_____

_____

_____

_____

_____

_____

_____

_____

Would you rank that Met Gala pizza party as one of Taylor's top five moments with her squad? List five of the most epic times she and her besties have had.

ONE _____

TWO _____

THREE _____

FOUR _____

FIVE _____

Behind every superstar is a dedicated fandom. Beyoncé has the Beyhive; Ariana Grande has the Arianators; Megan Thee Stallion has the Hotties; and Taylor, of course, has the Swifties. What does it truly mean to be a Swiftie?

Taylor's rendition of LeAnn Rimes's "Big Deal" helped her win a local talent show at age eleven. Which of Taylor's songs would you choose to sing if you ever performed at a talent competition?

SONG TITLE

CHAPTER FIVE

"FEARLESS"

AS TAYLOR'S FAME HAS GROWN, so has her "Fearless" spirit! Not only does she use her voice to speak out on issues that matter; she's a perfect example of what it looks like to gracefully stand up for yourself and others. In her *Fearless* album booklet, she wrote that the act of fearlessness is "getting back up and fighting for what you want over and over again." With that message in mind, think back to all the times when Taylor truly lived the definition of "brave." From clapping back at her enemies to attempting to dismantle the patriarchy through her music, this chapter puts the spotlight on Taylor's most fearless moments.

Taylor is the unofficial queen of clapbacks. Set a timer for one minute and jot down as many of her lyrical zingers as you can think of.

_____

_____

_____

_____

_____

_____

_____

_____

_____

_____

Now rank which five of those lines are your favorites!

ONE _____

TWO _____

THREE _____

FOUR _____

FIVE _____

Taylor has dealt with a lot while being in the public eye. Has she inspired you to face your own challenges head-on and overcome them while staying true to yourself? Give an example or two.

Kind, hardworking, and outspoken about issues that matter to her, Taylor is a role model to millions of fans around the world. When did she make you proudest to be a Swiftie?

_____

_____

_____

_____

_____

_____

_____

_____

_____

_____

Taylor always follows her heart and isn't afraid to do what's right, even if it makes her unpopular. What's the most fearless thing she's done?

_____

_____

_____

_____

_____

_____

_____

_____

_____

Taylor isn't one to stay silent for too long. What's the greatest battle—personal or professional—Taylor's ever fought and won? What did you learn from seeing her stand up for herself?

Negative press is part of the territory when you're as popular as Taylor, but she has a brilliant way of redirecting the attention back to her music. What do you think about Taylor's ability to ignore the haters and let her craft speak for itself?

Taylor seems to be in her most unbothered era yet, and it's so refreshing to watch! Case in point: changing up the lyrics to "Karma" to celebrate her relationship with Travis Kelce at one of the Eras Tour stops. Do you agree that Taylor's becoming more unapologetically herself in recent years? Why or why not?

What Netflix show did Taylor call out for its "lazy, deeply sexist joke" during Women's History Month in 2021?

A Ginny & Georgia

B Ginny & Madison

C Jimmy & Georgia

D Mickey & Georgia

My Answer

From "Mad Woman" and "I Did Something Bad" to "Lavender Haze" and, of course, "The Man," feminism is at the core of many of Taylor's tunes. Do you consider Taylor to be a feminist icon? Write down her most empowering lyrics.

Sometimes you have to fake it 'til you make it, right? Luckily, Taylor has lots of empowering words that can build you up when you're feeling down. Which song gives you the biggest confidence boost? Write down your favorite lyrics from the song.

SONG TITLE

Being kind to yourself and others can also feel empowering. What are the top five ways Taylor has spread good vibes to those around her?

1

2

3

4

5

Experimenting often comes with judgment and advice you didn't ask for—two things Taylor has dealt with firsthand—and it takes guts. Do you think Taylor experiments in a way that feels true to who she is as a person? Does it feel like a natural next step in her artistic evolution?

Taylor proves that writing from a vulnerable place is an act of bravery and strength. What has Taylor taught you about the importance of processing your emotions, good and bad?

Taylor donated to Kesha's legal expenses after a judge ruled against her request to record music outside her contract with producer Dr. Luke. How much did she donate?

A $100,000   C $250,000

B $200,000   D $350,000

My Answer

ANSWER C. Taylor "picks up the phone every time I call her," Kesha has said of Taylor's generosity.

Taylor has admitted that her understanding of the term "feminist" has changed since her teen years. How else do you think Taylor has evolved since her debut? What's the biggest shift you've noticed? Are you proud of her growth?

_____

_____

_____

_____

_____

_____

_____

_____

_____

Taylor sued a radio DJ who allegedly groped her in 2013 (winning a symbolic $1 verdict). She then made donations to charities that support sexual assault victims so their voices could also be heard. What message do you think the lawsuit sent to the music industry and to society as a whole?

_____

_____

_____

_____

_____

_____

_____

Early in her career, Taylor said she was advised against talking politics. Were you surprised when Taylor started to make her voice heard during the 2018 midterm elections? How do you think she handled the criticism of her political activism?

_____

_____

_____

_____

_____

_____

_____

_____

_____

Whether related to politics, women's rights, or other issues, write down five times Taylor stood up for something that stand out to you.

1 _____

2 _____

3 _____

4 _____

5 _____

Which member of Taylor's squad had these kind words to say about Taylor: "She's one of the people who is really supporting women in the entertainment business"?

A Selena Gomez

B Sarah Hyland

C Gigi Hadid

D Lorde

My Answer

Like her male and female counterparts, Taylor draws inspiration from her love life and pours those experiences into her music. Yet she seems to be criticized more than other artists for writing honestly about her past relationships! What's behind some of the unfair criticism? Do you think it's gotten better or worse over the years?

Fearless was the first album Taylor rerecorded as part of her masters dispute. She was just eighteen years old when *Fearless* came out in 2008. What's it like hearing "Love Story" and "Fifteen," along with deep cuts like "The Best Day" and "Change," sung from a more grown-up perspective? What about the "From the Vault" tracks? Do any of them resonate with you?

Taylor once said, "Grow a backbone, trust your gut, and know when to strike back. Be like a snake—only bite if someone steps on you." List five of Taylor's lyrics that best speak to inner strength.

1

2

3

4

5

Tough as nails, Taylor can always be counted on to rise above the drama! What's the best example of how she reclaimed the narrative and used it to her advantage?

In recent years, we've witnessed Taylor really own her power. For many, her journey toward independence is a beautiful representation of female empowerment. Do you agree? What's her most powerful message that speaks to this theme?

_____
_____
_____
_____
_____
_____
_____
_____
_____

Taylor refuses to compromise when it comes to the music she wants to create, whether it's honoring her country roots, going full-on pop, or bringing in hip-hop undertones. Which songs speak to her willingness to take risks and live by her own rules?

_____
_____
_____
_____
_____
_____
_____
_____

"You just have to live your life, and hopefully you'll take the right risks" is one of Taylor's most Instagram-worthy quotes. Which of Taylor's risks had the biggest payoff?

_____

_____

_____

_____

_____

_____

_____

_____

_____

How do you think the theme of empowerment will continue to present itself through Taylor's future projects? What do you hope to see more of?

_____

_____

_____

_____

_____

_____

_____

_____

Whether it's ignoring the haters or staying true to yourself, Taylor always seems to have the right words to say. Which quote didn't come from Taylor?

A "She lost him, but she found herself, and somehow that was everything."

B "Don't try to lessen yourself for the world; let the world catch up to you."

C "Happiness and confidence are two of the prettiest things you can wear."

D "Never believe anyone who says you don't deserve what you want."

My Answer

ANSWER B. These inspiring words were said by none other than Beyoncé, who Taylor thanked for paving "the road that every female artist is walking down now."

No matter how it's perceived, Taylor always does what's right for her. List the ways she empowers you to take greater control of your own life.

_____

_____

_____

_____

_____

_____

_____

_____

_____

_____

_____

Advocating for yourself in a male-dominated industry is a struggle for many female artists, but Taylor handles it with ease. What are some examples of how Taylor has shown you that she's truly a boss lady?

1 _____

2 _____

3 _____

4 _____

5 _____

CHAPTER SIX

"THE ALCHEMY"

MUSIC TRENDS COME AND GO, but it's safe to say that Taylor's songs will live on forever. In this chapter, let's look at Taylor's "it" factor, aka "The Alchemy." From headline-worthy business deals to her history-making wins, Taylor is an icon in every sense of the word! Accolades aside, Taylor's impact on the world is undeniable. As you flip through these upcoming pages, her most influential moments will remind you why she's an idol—both onstage and off.

From paying fans' rent and medical bills to bringing them to award shows as her plus-one, Taylor is often praised for how she engages with fans. Do you think Taylor's level of accessibility has rubbed off on other celebrities?

_____

_____

_____

_____

_____

_____

_____

_____

_____

Taylor brought hundreds of millions of dollars in brand value to the NFL while dating Travis Kelce. What's a cause you'd love to see get a boost from Taylor's influence? Why did you choose this issue? In what ways do you think it could benefit from the "Taylor Swift effect"?

CAUSE

_____

_____

_____

Many Swifties bought Travis Kelce's football jersey after his relationship with Taylor went public. What's his jersey number?

A 29   **C** 77

B 45   **D** 87

My Answer
_____

From overcoming blatant sexism to famous feuds, Taylor constantly proves that she controls her own narrative. What's an important lesson others can learn from watching Taylor?

_____

_____

_____

_____

_____

_____

_____

_____

_____

Taylor has been quoted as saying, "If you're lucky enough to be different, don't ever change." What's something about Taylor that you hope never changes?

_____

_____

_____

_____

_____

_____

_____

_____

Taylor lends a hand whenever she can, from supporting animal rights to quietly paying for a fan's student loans. How has she inspired you to give back?

From becoming the youngest artist to write and perform a number one hit on the *Billboard* Hot Country Songs chart to being the only artist to rake in $1 billion from a concert tour, it seems like Taylor smashes records every other week. Though impressive, do you think the awards and feats are really important? Why or why not?

_____

_____

_____

_____

_____

_____

_____

_____

_____

What are Taylor's top five contributions to the music industry? Is it her stellar songwriting? Her success in taking back her masters? What do you think she'll be most remembered for one hundred years from now?

ONE _____

TWO _____

THREE _____

FOUR _____

FIVE _____

For many Swifties, seeing a then-twenty-year-old Taylor win Album of the Year at the Grammys remains an unforgettable moment. Which career milestone do you remember most vividly?

_____

_____

_____

_____

_____

_____

_____

_____

_____

_____

Taylor has released a long string of albums since her 2006 debut. Which album do you think made Taylor an icon? In retrospect, what makes this album so special?

ALBUM TITLE

_____

_____

_____

_____

In what year did Taylor become the first and only person in Grammy history to win Album of the Year four times?

A 2009   **C** 2023

B 2015   **D** 2024

My Answer

ANSWER *D. She won Album of the Year at the Grammy Awards for Fearless, 1989, Folklore, and Midnights in 2010, 2016, 2021, and 2024, respectively.*

Taylor once shared that the gift that really excited her as a kid was a guitar. What is Taylor's greatest gift to the world?

Taylor was named *Billboard*'s first-ever Woman of the Decade for the 2010s. Compared with other artists in her age group, what makes her so special?

In 2019, the AMAs crowned Taylor Artist of the Decade. List ten of Taylor's career highlights that impress you the most.

1

2

3

4

5

6

7

8

9

10

You know you've arrived when a new millipede species, *Nannaria swiftae*, is named after you. If you could rename any existing species after Taylor, what would you come up with?

From pulling her music off Spotify to reclaiming her masters, Taylor is as business-savvy as they come. What's one business lesson all artists can learn from Taylor?

The trend of celebrities "going dark" on social media, especially Instagram, before a new project can be traced back to when Taylor announced *Reputation*'s album cover and release date. In what other ways has she pushed the music industry forward?

Taylor's got a heart of gold. Do you think her charity work and humanitarian efforts are overshadowed by her stardom? Write about her impact outside of music.

Much of Taylor's music is highly autobiographical. Who would you cast to play Taylor in her biopic if and when that day comes? Why did you choose this person?

Taylor deserves credit for offering a teen girl's perspective on country music. In retrospect, how do you feel about Taylor's recalibration from country to pop? Did you see it coming? How do you think it played a role in her staying power and overall impact?

_____

_____

_____

_____

_____

_____

_____

_____

_____

Taylor has been laser-focused on her rerecordings of her first six studio albums. What does this say about her dedication to her craft and achievement of artistic independence?

_____

_____

_____

_____

_____

_____

_____

_____

_____

?

Which one of Paul McCartney's songs (from his *Egypt Station* album) was inspired by Taylor?

(A) "I Don't Know"

(B) "Dominoes"

(C) "Confidante"

(D) "Who Cares"

My Answer

ANSWER D. In a BBC interview, McCartney said Taylor's relationship with her young fans inspired "Who Cares."

Whenever Taylor gets knocked down, she wastes no time dusting herself off and trying again! With Taylor rerecording her first six albums, do you believe it will inspire other artists, especially young women, to do the same? How do you think Taylor's act of taking ownership of the music she wrote will be viewed years from now?

Taylor certainly impacts her fans. But what sort of impact do you think the Swifties have on Taylor?

_____

_____

_____

_____

_____

_____

_____

_____

_____

Olivia Rodrigo said she's looked up to Taylor since the age of five, calling her the "best songwriter of all time." What other young artists appear to be influenced by Taylor? How has she laid the foundation for a new generation of singer-songwriters?

_____

_____

_____

_____

_____

_____

_____

_____

Which of Taylor's songs holds a Guinness World Record for fastest-selling digital single?

A "Shake It Off"

B "We Are Never Ever Getting Back Together"

C "Look What You Made Me Do"

D "Anti-Hero"

My Answer

Taylor's acceptance speeches are always thoughtful and sincere. She's given hundreds of them, but which speech do you think is the most inspirational? Why does it stand out?

From throwing shade at a certain someone who tried (and failed) to undercut her well-earned success to shouting out her fans for supporting the Equality Act, Taylor's speeches are almost as entertaining as the songs she writes. Which five speeches of Taylor's could you listen to over and over for instant motivation?

ONE

TWO

THREE

FOUR

FIVE

Kanye West interrupting Taylor as she accepted her Best Female Video award at the 2009 MTV VMAs will be remembered forever, but she handled it like a pro. How do you think that moment shaped Taylor professionally and personally?

The music industry is full of one-and-dones, but Taylor continues to prove she's in it for the long run. What's the secret behind her longevity?

Legendary artists like Carole King, Carly Simon, and Bruce Springsteen have given props to Taylor's songwriting. What are your favorite elements of her storytelling? Write down everything that comes to mind.

In the fall of 2022, Taylor released her highly anticipated tenth studio album, *Midnights*. What's your favorite song off the album? How do these songs compare to her previous works?

SONG TITLE

?

In what year did Taylor surpass Whitney Houston's record for the most AMA wins by a female artist?

A 2010   **C** 2018

B 2014   **D** 2020

My Answer

In 2010, Taylor received her own Madame Tussauds wax figure. So far, the figure has been showcased in Taylor's "Shake It Off" cheerleading costume, the blue sequin romper she wore at the 2019 iHeartRadio Music Awards, and more. Which one of Taylor's iconic looks do you want to see immortalized on her wax figure next?

From dropping Easter eggs to communicating in Morse code, Taylor and the Swifties clearly have their own language. Do you think Taylor's unique connection to her fans adds to her impact? Why or why not?

CHAPTER SEVEN

"SPEAK NOW"

THE WORLD'S BEST ARTISTS do more than just entertain—they motivate others to become better versions of themselves. This chapter invites you to "Speak Now" about the small (and big!) ways Taylor and her music inspire you day in and day out. From which songs bring you the most comfort on a bad day to the experiences you both have in common, let's focus on your personal connection to Taylor and her music.

Throughout her career, Taylor faced a double standard for writing honestly about her love life, a criticism she has deemed as "sexist." Is there a time when Taylor's unapologetic lyrics gave you the courage to tell your own story?

_____

_____

_____

_____

_____

_____

_____

_____

_____

Doing what you think is right is a powerful way to live. What are five examples Taylor has given you that showed what that looks like?

1 _____

2 _____

3 _____

4 _____

5 _____

Like many artists, Taylor copes with difficult emotions and situations by turning them into smash hits. Which of Taylor's songs do you find yourself turning to the most whenever you're having a terrible day? What is it about these lyrics that speak to you during those moments?

SONG TITLE

Taylor uses her platform, including acceptance speeches, to bring awareness to important issues like voting. How has she inspired you to become more involved in causes you're passionate about?

Look up some of Taylor's inspirational quotes, or think of lyrics you know that motivate you to do better and be better. Which are your top five?

1

2

3

4

5

Artists like Taylor hold the power to change people's lives through their music and the stories they share. In what ways has Taylor positively changed or influenced your life?

_____

_____

_____

_____

_____

_____

_____

_____

Taylor is the ultimate superstar. But when did you start to really appreciate Taylor as a human being? What made you see her in a different light?

_____

_____

_____

_____

_____

_____

_____

_____

Taylor tackles some universal topics in her music, such as heartbreak and bullying. Is there a song that feels like it was written specifically for you? What lines ring true to your experiences?

SONG TITLE

Taylor doesn't allow naysayers and critics to stop her from #winning and living life to the fullest. How has her resilience inspired you to turn adversity into opportunity?

Swifties know there's more to Taylor than just red carpet appearances, hit singles, and huge awards. What's one thing you wish everyone knew about Taylor?

From buying pizza for waiting fans to inviting them to her house and baking cookies for them, Taylor has to be one of the most down-to-earth celebrities. What qualities do you admire most about her?

Taylor once said that some of her lyrics contain zingers she wishes she could text people in real life. What's something you've always wanted to text someone? Write it down, then put it in lyric form.

ZINGER

_____

_____

_____

LYRICS

_____

_____

_____

_____

_____

_____

Taylor has stated that she felt like an outsider growing up because she didn't have any friends at school. Have you ever felt that way? Did Taylor's personal story and music help make you feel less alone?

_____

_____

_____

_____

_____

_____

_____

_____

_____

Taylor's *Lover* struck a chord with the LGBTQ+ community thanks to the "You Need to Calm Down" video and her "Me!" duet with Brendon Urie. When was the first time you felt validated by Taylor's storytelling—lyrically or visually? What did seeing that representation do for your sense of self?

The theme of self-reflection is front and center in Taylor's eighth album, *Folklore*. Have you ever experienced a personal breakthrough while listening to Taylor's music? What was the breakthrough?

_____

_____

_____

_____

_____

_____

_____

_____

Songs like "The Best Day," dedicated to Taylor's parents, and "The Man," which tackles double standards, are proof that not all of her music chronicles her romantic relationships. Which of her non-relationship songs is the most meaningful to you?

_____
SONG TITLE

_____

_____

_____

_____

?

Taylor's seventh studio album is famously titled *Lover*, but what was the project's original name?

A *Daylight* **C** *Afterglow*

B *Moonlight* **D** *Bliss*

My Answer

ANSWER A. On YouTube Live, Taylor shared that she "thought the title of this album was going to be Daylight for a couple months." That changed when she wrote the song "Lover."

Taylor's all for extending an olive branch whenever possible. Has Taylor ever inspired you to mend fences in your own life? Write about a situation when you took the high road and showed forgiveness despite feeling wronged.

During a sit-down interview with *CBS Sunday Morning*, Taylor admitted she's "the first to apologize when I'm wrong." Have you ever made a mistake that you owned up to? How did you feel afterward?

_____

_____

_____

_____

_____

_____

_____

_____

Owning up to your mistakes is definitely an admirable trait. What are five of Taylor's qualities that you respect?

ONE	
TWO	
THREE	
FOUR	
FIVE	

Taylor always seems to be challenging herself and trying new things. When was the last time you stepped outside your comfort zone? What did you learn about yourself during the process?

Upon its announcement, Taylor described *Midnights* as "the stories of 13 sleepless nights scattered throughout my life." If you wrote a collection of music in the middle of the night, what would you title it? What would it sound like? What stories would be revealed?

Taylor once said, "Being FEARLESS isn't being 100% Not FEARFUL, it's being terrified but you jump anyway." When is the last time you took a crazy chance? Was it a risk worth taking? What did you learn from it?

When Taylor and the legendary Stevie Nicks opened the 2010 Grammys, which of Fleetwood Mac's songs did they perform?

A "Gypsy"

B "Dreams"

C "Rhiannon"

D "Little Lies"

My Answer

Taylor shed her wholesome girl-next-door image with her concept album *Reputation*. Think about your reputation—what are you known for? How would your family and friends describe you?

Taylor always has the right words to say at the exact moment you need to hear them. Which one of her quotes do you find to be particularly moving? Did it change your outlook on a situation?

TAYLOR'S QUOTE

Ahead of *Lover*'s release in 2019, Taylor revealed that "Soon You'll Get Better," which chronicles her mother's illness, was the hardest song on the album to write. Thinking about your own life, which of Taylor's songs do you find hard to listen to? What difficult emotions are attached to it?

"The Outside" is about Taylor feeling like an outcast at school among her peers. In an interview with *Entertainment Weekly*, Taylor shared that "music has always been that escape." What's your escape when you feel misunderstood or when you're going through a rough time? Does Taylor's music help?

In 2020, Taylor honored her late grandmother, Marjorie Finlay, in the *Evermore* track "Marjorie." If you could honor one of your grandparents in the form of a song or poem, who would you choose and why? What do you admire most about them?

NAME

"I Can Do It with a Broken Heart" off *The Tortured Poets Department* is all about putting your best foot forward, even when you're hurting on the inside. When's the last time you had to do that? Are you good at compartmentalizing your emotions during challenging times? Why or why not?

_____

_____

_____

_____

_____

_____

_____

_____

_____

Taylor said, "I've never had an album where I needed songwriting more than I needed it on *Tortured Poets*." What's an album or song by Taylor that came at the perfect time for you? What was going on in your life? Did her music make it easier to handle?

```
╭─────────────────────────────────────╮
│                                       │
│                                       │
│           ALBUM OR SONG TITLE         │
╰─────────────────────────────────────╯
```

_____

_____

_____

_____

Taylor said that twenty-two was her "favorite year" due to the "carefree feeling that is sort of based on indecision and fear." What's been your favorite year of your life so far? What did it teach you?

_____

_____

_____

_____

_____

_____

_____

_____

_____

_____

During her "73 Questions" interview with *Vogue* in 2016, Taylor revealed that the letter she wrote to Apple Music rallying for artists to be fairly compensated is the bravest thing she thinks she's ever done. What's the most fearless thing you've ever done?

_____

_____

_____

_____

_____

_____

_____

_____

_____

?

When she was around fourteen, Taylor started modeling for which famous retailer?

A Hollister

B Aeropostale

C American Eagle

D Abercrombie & Fitch

My Answer

"Back to December" is notable because it was Taylor's first time apologizing to an ex in a song. Is there anyone you wish you could apologize to either through song, poetry, text, or face-to-face? What would you say to them? How do you think you may feel afterward?

Taylor has said being able to heal people would be an "amazing superpower." What would you choose as your superpower if you had one? How would you use it to better yourself and those around you?

It's nearly impossible not to get up and dance when "Shake It Off" is playing, but at its core, the upbeat track is all about you doing you and ignoring other people's opinions of you. When was the last time you had to shake it off?

Taylor wears her heart on her sleeve. For each song listed here, write down your favorite lines along with the specific emotions the song stirs up.

♪ "All Too Well"

♪ "Last Kiss"

♪ "Cruel Summer"

♪ "Getaway Car"

♪ "Champagne Problems"

♪ "Death by a Thousand Cuts"

♪ "Would've, Could've, Should've"

♪ "So Long, London"

PART

" *End Game* "

We've reached the "End Game," but the party's not over yet! Named after one of Taylor's catchiest singles, this part has lots of pages waiting to be transformed into your very own Taylor Swift coloring book and scrapbook. First, grab your colored pencils and fill in a log cabin in a forest, postcards of some key locations in Taylor lore, and the scales of a snake or wings of a butterfly. Then move on to the scrapbooking pages. That time when Taylor dressed as a purple squirrel for Halloween while quoting Megan Thee Stallion? Her priceless facial expressions at nearly every award show? Her sold-out Eras Tour concerts? Print or cut out your favorite photos and moments of Taylor, and paste them into the following pages so you can relive them over and over again.

TWO

ABOUT THE AUTHOR

PRINCESS GABBARA is a writer, editor, and pop culture enthusiast. Throughout Princess's versatile journalism career, her bylines have appeared across a host of print and digital publications, including Grammy.com, *Billboard*, *MTV News*, *Shondaland*, *Bustle*, *Oprah Daily*, *Vibe*, *Ebony*, and *Essence*. She is a graduate of Eastern Michigan University whose career highlights include exclusive interview coverage of celebrities including Mariah Carey, Jennifer Lopez, Babyface, Venus and Serena Williams, Lady Gaga, Mary J. Blige, Queen Latifah, Tracee Ellis Ross, Dionne Warwick, and Rita Moreno.

FOR EVERYONE WHO LOVES
THE BANGTAN BOYS!

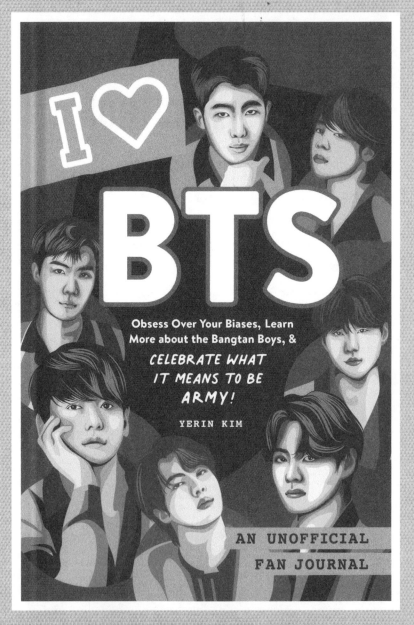